Elevate & Energize

50 Dynamic & Fun Activities for Peak Workplace Morale

Gerard Assey

Elevate & Energize:
50 Dynamic & Fun Activities for
Peak Workplace Morale
By
Gerard Assey
© Copyright 2024 by Author

Published by:
Gerard Assey
19/18, Palli Arasan Street
Anna Nagar East
Chennai - 600 102

ISBN: 978-81-967202-8-5

All Rights Reserved. No part of this publication may be reproduced, stored in a retrieval system, or transmitted in any form or by any means- electronic or mechanical, including photocopying, recording, or by any information storage and retrieval system, without prior written permission from the author.

(Image courtesy Freepik: 'https://www.freepik.com' Thank You)

Table of Contents

Preface

Welcome to "Elevate & Energize: 50 Dynamic & Fun Activities for Peak Workplace Morale." In the ever-evolving landscape of the professional world, the heartbeat of any successful organization lies in the morale and motivation of its workforce. This book is a testament to the understanding that a motivated, engaged, and enthusiastic team is not just a valuable asset; it is the very soul of a thriving workplace.

In the fast-paced rhythm of modern work life, it's easy for the vibrancy of the workplace to wane. Recognizing this, we embarked on a journey to curate a collection of activities that not only elevate spirits but also inject an infectious energy into the veins of your teams. "Elevate & Energize" is more than just a compilation; it is a playbook designed to catalyze positive change, foster camaraderie, and unleash the untapped potential within your organization.

As the title suggests, the heart of this book beats to the rhythm of dynamism and fun. Each activity within these pages is carefully crafted to be both impactful and enjoyable, ensuring that the pursuit of elevated morale becomes an adventure rather than a chore. We've tailored these activities to resonate with diverse teams, making them applicable across departments, from sales and marketing to production and beyond.

Behind every activity is a commitment to rejuvenating the workplace spirit. From desk decorating contests to team-building bingo, fitness challenges to gratitude walks, and DIY stress balls to office comedy hours, we've woven a tapestry of strategies that breathe life into the daily grind. These are not mere suggestions; they are invitations to create a workplace culture that thrives on positivity, creativity, and shared moments of joy.

Our hope is that this book becomes a well-worn companion for HR professionals and department heads alike, offering a go-to resource for infusing vitality into team dynamics. Consider it your guide to building not just teams but communities within your organization, where each member feels valued, inspired, and ready to contribute their best.

So, whether you're a seasoned HR professional seeking fresh inspiration or a departmental head yearning to invigorate your team, dive into "Elevate & Energize." May these pages be a source of inspiration, a catalyst for positive change, and a reminder that the journey to peak workplace morale is as fulfilling as the destination.

Let the elevation begin!

The Importance & Benefits of Morale Boosting Activities

Welcome to the foundational chapter of "Elevate & Energize: 50 Dynamic & Fun Activities for Peak Workplace Morale." Before we dive into the exciting world of morale-boosting activities, let's explore why investing time and effort in these endeavors is more than just a good idea—it's a strategic imperative for any thriving organization.

The Heartbeat of Workplace Morale

In the heartbeat of every organization, you'll find its people. They are not merely cogs in the machinery of tasks; they are the soul that breathes life into every project, every goal, and every success. Workplace morale, often described as the collective mood, spirit, and attitude of a team, is the undercurrent that shapes the overall health and productivity of an organization.

Why is it Important?

- ✓ **Productivity Amplification:** High morale is the secret sauce that amplifies productivity. Engaged and motivated employees bring their best selves to work, leading to increased efficiency and better output.
- ✓ **Talent Retention and Attraction:** In a competitive job market, attracting and retaining top talent is a constant challenge. A positive work culture, fueled by high morale, becomes a magnet for talent.
- ✓ **Innovation and Problem-Solving:** Teams with elevated morale are more likely to collaborate, share ideas, and engage in creative problem-solving. Innovation thrives in

an atmosphere of positivity and mutual respect.

- ✓ **Resilience in Challenges:** A team with high morale is better equipped to navigate challenges. When faced with setbacks, they approach problems with a solutions-oriented mindset, drawing strength from their collective spirit.
- ✓ **Customer Satisfaction:** Happy employees contribute to satisfied customers. The positive energy radiating from a motivated team often extends to client interactions, enhancing customer satisfaction.

The Benefits Unveiled

Now that we understand the importance, let's unravel the specific benefits these morale-boosting activities bring to the table.

1. Enhanced Team Building: Morale-boosting activities create shared experiences, fostering a sense of unity and camaraderie among team members. These shared moments contribute to the formation of a cohesive and collaborative team.

2. Increased Employee Engagement: Engaged employees are emotionally committed to their work. Morale-boosting activities provide avenues for personal connection, making employees feel valued and engaged in their professional journey.

3. Stress Reduction: The modern workplace can be stressful. Morale-boosting activities act as pressure valves, allowing employees to release stress and rejuvenate their minds, contributing to overall mental well-being.

4. Boosted Creativity: Fun and dynamic activities stimulate creative thinking. When employees are encouraged to think outside the box in a relaxed setting, it translates into innovative solutions within the workplace.

5. Positive Cultural Impact: A workplace with high morale exudes positivity. This positive atmosphere becomes embedded in the organizational culture, influencing how employees interact, communicate, and approach challenges.

6. Improved Morale, Improved Performance: It's a cyclical relationship—elevated morale leads to improved performance, and improved performance contributes to sustained high morale. These activities set the wheels of this positive cycle in motion.

In the chapters to come, we'll explore 50 activities carefully curated to tap into these benefits. Each activity is a step toward creating a workplace where morale is not just a metric but a living, breathing entity that propels your organization to new heights.

Are you ready to embark on the journey of workplace transformation? Let's dive in and elevate your team's morale to unprecedented heights.

How to Use This Book - A Step-by-Step Plan

Congratulations on choosing "Elevate & Energize: 50 Dynamic & Fun Activities for Peak Workplace Morale" as your guide to transforming your workplace culture! This chapter is designed to be your roadmap, offering a step-by-step plan on how to make the most of the activities presented in this book.

Step 1: Assess Your Team's Needs

Before diving into the activities, take a moment to assess your team's current dynamics. Consider factors such as:

- ✓ Current Morale Levels: Reflect on the overall mood and morale of your team. Are there specific challenges or areas that need attention?
- ✓ Team Dynamics: Understand the existing relationships and communication patterns within your team. Are there any gaps or opportunities for improvement?
- ✓ Workplace Environment: Consider the physical and cultural aspects of your workplace. How can these activities be tailored to suit your unique setting?

Step 2: Set Clear Objectives

Define what you aim to achieve with these activities. Your objectives might include:

- ✓ Boosting Team Morale: Enhance the overall mood and spirit within the team.
- ✓ Improving Communication: Foster better communication and collaboration among team members.

- ✓ Celebrating Milestones: Acknowledge achievements and milestones in a meaningful way.
- ✓ Enhancing Creativity: Stimulate creative thinking and problem-solving skills.
- ✓ Building Team Unity: Strengthen the sense of unity and camaraderie among team members.

Step 3: Tailor Activities to Your Team

While the activities presented in this book are versatile, feel free to tailor them to suit your team's preferences and work environment. Consider factors such as:

- ✓ Team Size: Adapt activities based on the size of your team.
- ✓ Work Setting: Modify activities to align with your office layout or remote work dynamics.
- ✓ Team Preferences: Consider the unique interests and preferences of your team members.

Step 4: Plan Activities Strategically

To ensure the success of these morale-boosting activities, plan strategically:

- ✓ Frequency: Determine how often you'll implement these activities. Regular, consistent engagement is key.
- ✓ Timing: Schedule activities at times that won't disrupt essential work tasks. Lunch breaks, Fridays, or designated team-building days can be ideal.
- ✓ Integration: Integrate activities seamlessly into your team's workflow to make them an organic part of the workplace culture.

Step 5: Identify Appropriate Moments

Knowing when to implement these activities is crucial. Consider using them during:

✓ Transition Periods: Introduce activities during times of change or transition to maintain a positive atmosphere.
✓ After Achievements: Celebrate successes and milestones with morale-boosting activities.
✓ Regular Check-ins: Use activities as part of regular check-ins to maintain ongoing team engagement.
✓ Periods of Stress: Introduce stress-relief activities during demanding work periods.

Step 6: Evaluate and Adjust

After implementing activities, gather feedback and evaluate their impact. Consider:

✓ Feedback Sessions: Encourage team members to share their thoughts and feelings about each activity.
✓ Observations: Observe changes in team dynamics, communication, and overall mood.
✓ Adjustments: Be open to adjusting activities based on feedback and evolving team needs.

Step 7: Document and Share Success Stories

Celebrate the success of these activities by documenting and sharing positive outcomes. Highlight:

✓ Success Stories: Share anecdotes and success stories from each activity.
✓ Impact on Morale: Showcase how these activities have positively influenced team morale.
✓ Continuous Improvement: Use feedback and success stories to continually refine and improve your approach.

By following these steps, you'll not only make the most of the activities presented in this book but also establish a framework for an ongoing, positive, and engaging workplace culture.

Are you ready to embark on this transformative journey? Let's elevate and energize your workplace together!

Assessing Team's Needs for Morale Boosting:
A Step-by-Step Method

Step 1: Define the Purpose of the Assessment
Clearly outline the objectives of the assessment. Consider aspects such as understanding current morale levels, identifying challenges, and pinpointing opportunities for improvement.

Step 2: Gather Relevant Data
Collect both quantitative and qualitative data to gain a comprehensive understanding of the team dynamics. Utilize methods such as surveys, interviews, and focus group discussions.

Step 3: Choose Assessment Criteria
Identify key criteria that align with the overall objectives. This could include:

- ✓ Communication and Collaboration
- ✓ Job Satisfaction
- ✓ Work-Life Balance
- ✓ Recognition and Appreciation
- ✓ Team Dynamics

Step 4: Design Assessment Tools
Create assessment tools that align with chosen criteria. These tools can include:

- ✓ Surveys: Develop a questionnaire with a mix of rating scales and open-ended questions.
- ✓ Interviews: Conduct one-on-one or group interviews to gather in-depth insights.
- ✓ Focus Groups: Facilitate discussions with a diverse group to capture varied perspectives.

Step 5: Administer the Assessment

Implement the assessment tools, ensuring confidentiality and anonymity to encourage honest feedback. Use a combination of methods for a holistic view.

Step 6: Analyze Data

Evaluate the collected data to identify patterns, trends, and areas of concern. Look for both strengths and weaknesses within the team.

Step 7: Identify Key Findings

Summarize key findings from the analysis. These could include standout positive aspects, areas requiring attention, and potential root causes of morale issues.

Step 8: Prioritize Areas for Improvement

Rank the identified areas based on their impact and feasibility for improvement. This prioritization will guide the development of targeted morale-boosting strategies.

Step 9: Develop Actionable Recommendations

Translate the findings into actionable recommendations. These could range from implementing specific morale-boosting activities to addressing systemic issues within the organization.

Step 10: Create an Implementation Plan

Outline a step-by-step plan for implementing the recommended strategies. Define roles, responsibilities, and timelines to ensure a smooth execution.

Template for Team Morale Assessment:

1. Objective of the Assessment: Clearly state the purpose and objectives of the assessment.

2. Assessment Criteria: Identify the key criteria you will focus on.

Examples include Communication, Collaboration, Job Satisfaction, Work-Life Balance, Recognition, and Team Dynamics.

3. Assessment Tools:

- ✓ Survey Questions:
  Develop a mix of rating scales (e.g., on a scale of 1 to 5) and open-ended questions.
- ✓ Interview Guides:
  Create a set of questions for one-on-one or group interviews.
- ✓ Focus Group Plan:
  Outline the structure and topics for focus group discussions.

4. Administration:

- ✓ Specify the timeline for the assessment.
- ✓ Detail the method of data collection (e.g., online surveys, in-person interviews).

5. Data Analysis:

- ✓ Describe the process of data analysis, including tools or software used.
- ✓ Highlight how you'll identify patterns, trends, and key insights.

6. Key Findings:

- ✓ Summarize the main discoveries from the data analysis.
- ✓ Highlight positive aspects and areas for improvement.

7. Prioritization:

Rank the identified areas based on their impact and feasibility for improvement.

8. Recommendations:

- ✓ Translate findings into actionable recommendations.
- ✓ Provide a rationale for each recommendation.

9. Implementation Plan:

✓ Outline a step-by-step plan for implementing recommendations.
✓ Include roles, responsibilities, and timelines.

10. Follow-Up:
✓ Specify how you'll monitor and evaluate the impact of implemented strategies.
✓ Include plans for periodic reassessment to track ongoing team dynamics.

This template provides a structured approach to assessing team morale, ensuring that the process is comprehensive, actionable, and focused on continuous improvement.

1. Desk Decorating Contest

Objective:
- ✓ Foster creativity and personalization in the workplace.
- ✓ Boost team morale by showcasing individual personalities.
- ✓ Create a positive and vibrant work environment.

Materials Required:
- ✓ Decorating supplies (colored paper, markers, stickers, etc.).
- ✓ Prizes for winners (can be small and fun, such as gift cards or office supplies).

Timing:
- ✓ Monthly, with a set day for judging.

How to conduct the activity:
- ✓ Announce the contest at the beginning of the month, providing guidelines and themes if any.
- ✓ Allow employees the entire month to decorate their desks.
- ✓ Designate a day for judging, where a panel or the entire team votes for the most creatively decorated desk.
- ✓ Announce the winners and award prizes.

Trainer Observations:
- ✓ Observe the level of creativity in each decoration.
- ✓ Note how employees incorporate personal touches into their workspaces.
- ✓ Pay attention to the overall impact on the office atmosphere.

Prompting Discussion:

- ✓ Discuss the creative process with participants.
- ✓ Encourage them to share the inspiration behind their decorations.
- ✓ Facilitate a conversation about the impact of a personalized workspace on morale.

Application/Learning:

- ✓ Encourages creative expression.
- ✓ Enhances team bonding through shared experiences.
- ✓ Promotes a positive and enjoyable work environment.

2. Themed Dress-Up Days

Objective:
- ✓ Inject fun and creativity into the workweek.
- ✓ Build team spirit through shared participation.
- ✓ Provide a break from routine and boost morale.

Materials Required:
- ✓ None, unless specific themes require certain props or costumes.

Timing:
- ✓ Weekly or bi-monthly, depending on team preferences.

How to conduct the activity:
- ✓ Announce the theme in advance.
- ✓ Encourage employees to dress up according to the theme on the designated day.
- ✓ Optionally, organize a brief parade or fashion show for participants to showcase their costumes.
- ✓ Take photos for a fun recap or future reference.

Trainer Observations:
- ✓ Observe participation levels.
- ✓ Note creativity and effort put into costumes.
- ✓ Assess the overall impact on team dynamics.

Prompting Discussion:
- ✓ Discuss the choice of costumes and the thought process behind them.
- ✓ Encourage participants to share funny or interesting anecdotes related to their outfits.
- ✓ Facilitate a conversation about the positive impact on team morale.

Application/Learning:
- ✓ Fosters creativity and individual expression.
- ✓ Strengthens team bonds through shared experiences.
- ✓ Provides a lighthearted break from the routine.

3. Team Building Bingo

Objective:
- ✓ Promote team collaboration and communication.
- ✓ Encourage employees to interact with colleagues from different departments.
- ✓ Foster a sense of unity through shared activities.

Materials Required:
- ✓ Bingo cards with team-building activities.
- ✓ Pens or markers.

Timing:
- ✓ Weekly or monthly, depending on the frequency desired.

How to conduct the activity:
- ✓ Distribute Bingo cards to employees.
- ✓ Explain the rules and objectives of the game.
- ✓ Participants complete activities on the Bingo card, marking them off as they go.
- ✓ The first person to complete a row or column shouts "Bingo" and wins a prize.

Trainer Observations:
- ✓ Observe collaboration during team-building activities.
- ✓ Note the level of interaction between colleagues from different departments.
- ✓ Assess the overall enthusiasm and engagement.

Prompting Discussion:
- ✓ Discuss the challenges and successes participants faced during the activities.

- ✓ Encourage conversations about newfound connections and interactions.
- ✓ Facilitate a discussion on the importance of cross-departmental collaboration.

Application/Learning:
- ✓ Strengthens teamwork and collaboration skills.
- ✓ Encourages networking and relationship-building.
- ✓ Reinforces the importance of a unified workplace.

4. Recognition Wall

Objective:
- ✓ Cultivate a culture of appreciation and gratitude.
- ✓ Boost morale by acknowledging and celebrating individual and team achievements.
- ✓ Strengthen the sense of community within the workplace.

Materials Required:
- ✓ Bulletin board or designated wall space.
- ✓ Sticky notes, markers, and pins.

Timing:
- ✓ Ongoing, with regular reviews and updates.

How to conduct the activity:
- ✓ Designate a space for the Recognition Wall.
- ✓ Encourage employees to write notes recognizing their colleagues for their hard work.
- ✓ Provide markers, sticky notes, and pins for employees to post their messages.
- ✓ Regularly review the wall and celebrate achievements as a team.

Trainer Observations:
- ✓ Observe the frequency of updates on the Recognition Wall.
- ✓ Note the variety and sincerity of messages.
- ✓ Assess the overall impact on workplace culture.

Prompting Discussion:
- ✓ Discuss the positive effects of acknowledgment on morale.

- ✓ Encourage employees to share stories of when they felt appreciated.
- ✓ Facilitate a conversation about the importance of recognizing and celebrating achievements.

Application/Learning:

- ✓ Cultivates a positive and appreciative workplace culture.
- ✓ Strengthens team bonds through acknowledgment.
- ✓ Promotes a sense of community and shared success.

5. Fitness Challenge

Objective:
- ✓ Promote employee well-being and a healthy lifestyle.
- ✓ Encourage team collaboration and friendly competition.
- ✓ Boost morale through shared fitness goals.

Materials Required:
- ✓ Fitness tracking tools or apps.
- ✓ Prizes for the most active team.

Timing:
- ✓ Month-long, with regular check-ins and updates.

How to conduct the activity:
- ✓ Divide employees into teams.
- ✓ Set daily or weekly fitness goals for each team.
- ✓ Use fitness tracking tools or apps to monitor progress.
- ✓ Award prizes to the team that achieves the most fitness goals.

Trainer Observations:
- ✓ Monitor participation levels and enthusiasm.
- ✓ Observe team dynamics and collaboration during the challenge.
- ✓ Assess the overall impact on individual well-being.

Prompting Discussion:
- ✓ Discuss the positive effects of regular exercise on well-being.
- ✓ Encourage employees to share their fitness journey and challenges.

  - ✓ Facilitate a conversation about incorporating healthy habits into the workplace.

Application/Learning:

  - ✓ Promotes a healthy and active lifestyle.
  - ✓ Strengthens team bonds through shared goals.
  - ✓ Reinforces the importance of well-being in the workplace.

6. DIY Wellness Day

Objective:
- ✓ Prioritize employee well-being by providing a day dedicated to mental and physical wellness.
- ✓ Introduce and encourage healthy practices such as yoga, meditation, and cooking.
- ✓ Foster a positive and relaxed atmosphere in the workplace.

Materials Required:
- ✓ Yoga mats, meditation cushions, or blankets.
- ✓ A quiet and comfortable space for wellness activities.
- ✓ Ingredients for healthy cooking classes.

Timing:
- ✓ One full workday, preferably scheduled on a less hectic day.

How to conduct the activity:
Start the day with a group yoga session or meditation.
- ✓ Organize wellness workshops or classes throughout the day, including healthy cooking classes.
- ✓ Allow employees to choose which sessions to attend.
- ✓ Encourage breaks for mindful walks or stretching exercises.

Trainer Observations:
- ✓ Observe participation levels in each wellness activity.
- ✓ Note the atmosphere and mood throughout the day.

- ✓ Assess the overall impact on employees' well-being.

Prompting Discussion:
- ✓ Discuss the importance of incorporating wellness activities into the work routine.
- ✓ Encourage employees to share their experiences and favorite activities.
- ✓ Facilitate a conversation about integrating wellness practices into daily life.

Application/Learning:
- ✓ Promotes a healthy work-life balance.
- ✓ Provides practical tools for stress management.
- ✓ Encourages mindfulness and well-being in the workplace.

7. Mystery Lunch Pals

Objective:
- ✓ Foster connections and relationships among employees.
- ✓ Encourage social interaction in a fun and informal setting.
- ✓ Build a sense of camaraderie and understanding within the team.

Materials Required:
- ✓ A system for randomly pairing employees.
- ✓ Communication platform for revealing lunch pals at the end of the month.

Timing:
- ✓ One month, with lunch dates coordinated by participants.

How to conduct the activity:
- ✓ Randomly pair employees at the beginning of the month.
- ✓ Instruct participants to have lunch together at least once a week.
- ✓ Encourage participants not to reveal their identities until the end of the month.
- ✓ At the end of the month, host a casual gathering to reveal lunch pals.

Trainer Observations:
- ✓ Observe the frequency of participation in lunch dates.
- ✓ Note the level of engagement and enjoyment expressed by participants.
- ✓ Assess the impact on team relationships.

Prompting Discussion:

- ✓ Discuss the experience of getting to know a colleague in a casual setting.
- ✓ Encourage employees to share interesting or surprising discoveries about their lunch pals.
- ✓ Facilitate a conversation about the importance of building connections at work.

Application/Learning:

- ✓ Strengthens interpersonal relationships within the team.
- ✓ Encourages cross-functional understanding.
- ✓ Promotes a positive and friendly workplace culture.

8. Escape Room Challenge

Objective:
- ✓ Enhance problem-solving and collaboration skills in a fun and challenging setting.
- ✓ Foster teamwork and communication among employees.
- ✓ Provide an enjoyable and memorable team-building experience.

Materials Required
- ✓ Booking at an escape room venue.
- ✓ Transportation to the venue if necessary.

Timing:
- ✓ Half-day or full-day, depending on the complexity of the escape room.

How to conduct the activity:
- ✓ Book a session at an escape room venue.
- ✓ Divide employees into teams.
- ✓ Provide instructions and rules before entering the escape room.
- ✓ Debrief after the activity, discussing teamwork and problem-solving strategies.

Trainer Observations:
- ✓ Observe teamwork dynamics within each group.
- ✓ Note communication patterns during the challenge.
- ✓ Assess the overall enjoyment and engagement.

Prompting Discussion:
- ✓ Discuss the challenges faced during the escape room challenge.

- ✓ Encourage teams to share their strategies for problem-solving.
- ✓ Facilitate a conversation about the application of teamwork skills in the workplace.

Application/Learning:

- ✓ Strengthens problem-solving and collaboration skills.
- ✓ Encourages effective communication.
- ✓ Provides a memorable and enjoyable team-building experience.

9. Office Olympics

Objective:
- ✓ Infuse energy and fun into the workplace through light-hearted competitions.
- ✓ Foster friendly competition and teamwork.
- ✓ Enhance team spirit and morale.

Materials Required:
- ✓ Office supplies for games (chairs, paper for airplanes, etc.).
- ✓ Prizes for the winners.

Timing:
- ✓ Half-day or full-day, scheduled during a suitable time.

How to conduct the activity:
- ✓ Plan a variety of office-friendly games (chair races, paper airplane contests, desk chair spinning, etc.).
- ✓ Divide employees into teams.
- ✓ Rotate through the games with a scoring system.
- ✓ Award prizes to the winning team.

Trainer Observations:
- ✓ Observe teamwork and sportsmanship during each game.
- ✓ Note creativity and engagement levels.
- ✓ Assess the overall impact on team dynamics.

Prompting Discussion:
- ✓ Discuss the most enjoyable moments of the Office Olympics.
- ✓ Encourage teams to share their strategies and experiences.

- ✓ Facilitate a conversation about the importance of friendly competition and teamwork.

Application/Learning:

- ✓ Enhances team spirit and camaraderie.
- ✓ Provides a break from routine and boosts morale.
- ✓ Fosters creativity and teamwork.

10. Skill Share Sessions

Objective:
- ✓ Promote a culture of continuous learning and personal development.
- ✓ Facilitate knowledge sharing among employees.
- ✓ Strengthen team bonds through shared interests and skills.

Materials Required:
- ✓ Meeting room or common space for sessions.
- ✓ A schedule for employees to sign up for hosting sessions.

Timing:
- ✓ Regularly scheduled sessions, such as bi-monthly or monthly.

How to conduct the activity:
- ✓ Invite employees to sign up to host skill share sessions.
- ✓ Topics can range from professional skills to personal hobbies.
- ✓ Host the sessions in a relaxed and informal setting.
- ✓ Encourage participants to ask questions and engage in discussions.

Trainer Observations:
- ✓ Observe the level of engagement during each session.
- ✓ Note the variety and relevance of topics.
- ✓ Assess the impact on team learning and bonding.

Prompting Discussion:

- ✓ Discuss the value of continuous learning and skill-sharing.
- ✓ Encourage participants to share their takeaways from each session.
- ✓ Facilitate a conversation about the application of new skills in the workplace.

Application/Learning:

- ✓ Fosters a culture of continuous learning.
- ✓ Strengthens team bonds through shared experiences.
- ✓ Promotes personal and professional development.

11. Positive Affirmation Cards

Objective:
- ✓ Cultivate a positive and supportive workplace culture.
- ✓ Boost morale by spreading positivity and encouragement.
- ✓ Foster a mindset of self-affirmation among employees.

Materials Required:
- ✓ Positive affirmation cards or small cards to write motivational quotes.
- ✓ Pens or markers.

Timing:
- ✓ Ongoing, with cards distributed periodically.

How to conduct the activity:
- ✓ Provide employees with positive affirmation cards or encourage them to create their own.
- ✓ Distribute the cards at the beginning of the week or during team meetings.
- ✓ Encourage employees to keep the cards on their desks or in a visible place.
- ✓ Periodically introduce new affirmations or quotes to keep the positive energy flowing.

Trainer Observations:
- ✓ Observe the atmosphere in the workplace.
- ✓ Note any changes in employee morale or attitude.
- ✓ Assess the overall impact on the workplace culture.

Prompting Discussion:
- ✓ Discuss the importance of maintaining a positive mindset.

- ✓ Encourage employees to share their favorite affirmations.
- ✓ Facilitate a conversation about the role of positivity in the workplace.

Application/Learning:

- ✓ Cultivates a positive and encouraging workplace culture.
- ✓ Promotes a mindset of self-affirmation.
- ✓ Enhances overall employee morale.

12. Secret Santa Desk Surprises

Objective:
- ✓ Spread joy and build a sense of camaraderie.
- ✓ Create a positive and festive atmosphere in the workplace.
- ✓ Encourage small acts of kindness among colleagues.

Materials Required:
- ✓ Small gifts, notes, or tokens of appreciation.
- ✓ A system for assigning Secret Santas.

Timing:
- ✓ One week, preferably during a festive season or holiday.

How to conduct the activity:
- ✓ Assign each participant a Secret Santa.
- ✓ Set a budget for gifts to ensure affordability.
- ✓ Encourage participants to leave small surprises or notes on their assigned colleague's desk throughout the week.
- ✓ Reveal the Secret Santas at the end of the week, optionally during a team gathering.

Trainer Observations:
- ✓ Observe the overall atmosphere during the week.
- ✓ Note the creativity and thoughtfulness of the surprises.
- ✓ Assess the impact on team morale and connections.

Prompting Discussion:
- ✓ Discuss the experience of being a Secret Santa or receiving surprises.

- ✓ Encourage participants to share memorable moments from the week.
- ✓ Facilitate a conversation about the importance of kindness in the workplace.

Application/Learning:

- ✓ Fosters a positive and festive workplace atmosphere.
- ✓ Encourages acts of kindness and appreciation.
- ✓ Strengthens team connections and camaraderie.

13. Coffee Break Networking

Objective:
- ✓ Facilitate cross-departmental connections and networking.
- ✓ Break down silos and encourage a more integrated workplace.
- ✓ Create opportunities for employees to get to know one another.

Materials Required:
- ✓ Coffee or refreshments.
- ✓ A designated space for coffee breaks.

Timing:
- ✓ Regularly scheduled, such as bi-monthly or monthly.

How to conduct the activity:
- ✓ Schedule short coffee breaks during which employees are encouraged to mingle.
- ✓ Choose a central location for the breaks to promote interaction.
- ✓ Use icebreaker activities or conversation starters if needed.
- ✓ Rotate employees to different coffee break groups periodically.

Trainer Observations:
- ✓ Observe the level of participation and engagement.
- ✓ Note the diversity of interactions between employees.
- ✓ Assess the overall impact on cross-departmental connections.

Prompting Discussion:

- ✓ Discuss the benefits of cross-departmental networking.
- ✓ Encourage employees to share interesting conversations or connections made.
- ✓ Facilitate a conversation about the importance of collaboration across departments.

Application/Learning:

- ✓ Fosters cross-departmental connections.
- ✓ Encourages a more integrated workplace.
- ✓ Promotes a sense of unity and understanding.

14. Employee of the Month Podcast

Objective:
- ✓ Celebrate and recognize outstanding employees.
- ✓ Showcase individual achievements and contributions.
- ✓ Boost morale by sharing success stories within the organization.

Materials Required:
- ✓ Recording equipment or a platform for creating podcasts.
- ✓ A list of questions for the interview.

Timing:
- ✓ Monthly, with the podcast released at the end of each month.

How to conduct the activity:
- ✓ Select an outstanding employee to feature each month.
- ✓ Conduct an interview-style podcast, discussing their achievements and experiences.
- ✓ Edit and produce the podcast for release.
- ✓ Share the podcast internally or on a company platform.

Trainer Observations:
- ✓ Observe the impact of the podcast on employee morale.
- ✓ Note the engagement levels and feedback from employees.
- ✓ Assess the overall atmosphere in the workplace.

Prompting Discussion:

- ✓ Discuss the achievements and experiences highlighted in the podcast.
- ✓ Encourage employees to share their thoughts and reflections.
- ✓ Facilitate a conversation about the importance of recognizing and celebrating achievements.

Application/Learning:

- ✓ Boosts morale through positive recognition.
- ✓ Showcases individual achievements within the organization.
- ✓ Promotes a culture of celebrating success.

15. Charity Team Building

Objective:
- ✓ Promote teamwork and collaboration through charitable activities.
- ✓ Contribute to a meaningful cause and foster a sense of social responsibility.
- ✓ Strengthen team bonds through shared experiences.

Materials Required:
- ✓ Depending on the activity: volunteering supplies, materials for a charity run, etc.
- ✓ Information about the chosen charitable cause.

Timing:
- ✓ Half-day or full-day, depending on the chosen activity.

How to conduct the activity:
- ✓ Choose a charitable activity, such as volunteering or organizing a charity run.
- ✓ Organize teams and provide necessary information about the chosen cause.
- ✓ Execute the charity team-building activity.
- ✓ Debrief afterward, discussing the impact and lessons learned.

Trainer Observations:
- ✓ Observe teamwork and collaboration during the charitable activity.
- ✓ Note the level of engagement and enthusiasm.
- ✓ Assess the overall impact on team dynamics and social responsibility.

Prompting Discussion:

✓ Discuss the chosen charitable cause and its significance.
✓ Encourage teams to share their experiences during the activity.
✓ Facilitate a conversation about the importance of giving back to the community.

Application/Learning:
✓ Strengthens teamwork and collaboration skills.
✓ Fosters a sense of social responsibility.
✓ Provides a meaningful and impactful team-building experience.

16. Personal Development Book Club

Objective:
- ✓ Promote continuous learning and personal development.
- ✓ Foster a culture of shared knowledge and insights.
- ✓ Provide a platform for employees to apply learnings to their personal and professional lives.

Materials Required:
- ✓ Copies of the selected personal development book.
- ✓ A designated meeting space or a virtual platform for discussions.

Timing:
- ✓ Monthly or bi-monthly, depending on the length and complexity of the chosen book.

How to conduct the activity:
- ✓ Choose a personal development book for each session.
- ✓ Announce the book club and encourage employees to participate.
- ✓ Set a schedule for regular meetings to discuss the book.
- ✓ Facilitate discussions by asking open-ended questions and encouraging participants to share insights and personal applications.

Trainer Observations:
- ✓ Observe participation levels during book club meetings.
- ✓ Note the depth and variety of insights shared.

- ✓ Assess the overall impact on participants' personal development.

Prompting Discussion:
- ✓ Discuss the key takeaways and learnings from each book.
- ✓ Encourage participants to share how they've applied insights in their lives.
- ✓ Facilitate conversations about personal growth and development.

Application/Learning:
- ✓ Encourages continuous learning and reading.
- ✓ Provides a platform for sharing and applying knowledge.
- ✓ Fosters a culture of personal and professional development.

17. DIY Art Exhibition

Objective:
- ✓ Showcase and celebrate employees' artistic talents.
- ✓ Create a positive and vibrant work environment.
- ✓ Encourage creativity and self-expression.

Materials Required:
- ✓ Art supplies (canvases, paint, markers, etc.).
- ✓ Display boards or designated areas for showcasing artwork.

Timing:
- ✓ Half-day or full-day, scheduled during a suitable time.

How to conduct the activity:
- ✓ Announce the DIY art exhibition and invite participants.
- ✓ Provide art supplies and a designated space for employees to create their artwork.
- ✓ Set a date for the exhibition where employees can showcase their pieces.
- ✓ Encourage participants to share the inspiration behind their artwork during the exhibition.

Trainer Observations:
- ✓ Observe the variety and creativity of the artwork.
- ✓ Note the level of employee engagement and enthusiasm.
- ✓ Assess the impact on the workplace atmosphere.

Prompting Discussion:

- ✓ Discuss the stories and inspirations behind each piece of art.
- ✓ Encourage participants to share their artistic processes.
- ✓ Facilitate conversations about the role of creativity in the workplace.

Application/Learning:

- ✓ Celebrates individual creativity and self-expression.
- ✓ Enhances the workplace environment with visual art.
- ✓ Fosters a culture that values and appreciates artistic talents.

18. Office Trivia Night

Objective:
- ✓ Provide a fun and interactive team-building activity.
- ✓ Foster a sense of camaraderie and friendly competition.
- ✓ Promote knowledge about the company's history, industry, and colleagues.

Materials Required:
- ✓ Trivia questions related to the company, industry, and fun facts about colleagues.
- ✓ A designated space for the trivia night.

Timing:
- ✓ Evening event, scheduled during a convenient time.

How to conduct the activity:
- ✓ Prepare a set of trivia questions covering company history, industry knowledge, and fun facts about colleagues.
- ✓ Divide employees into teams.
- ✓ Host the trivia night, asking questions and keeping score.
- ✓ Award prizes to the winning team.

Trainer Observations:
- ✓ Observe teamwork and collaboration during the trivia night.
- ✓ Note the level of engagement and enthusiasm.
- ✓ Assess the overall impact on team dynamics.

Prompting Discussion:
- ✓ Discuss the trivia questions and the knowledge shared.

- ✓ Encourage teams to share their strategies for answering questions.
- ✓ Facilitate conversations about the importance of fun activities in the workplace.

Application/Learning:

- ✓ Fosters a sense of camaraderie through friendly competition.
- ✓ Promotes knowledge-sharing about the company and colleagues.
- ✓ Provides a lighthearted and enjoyable team-building experience.

19. Gratitude Jar

Objective:
- ✓ Cultivate a culture of gratitude and appreciation.
- ✓ Boost morale by acknowledging and celebrating small victories.
- ✓ Strengthen team bonds through positive affirmations.

Materials Required:
- ✓ A decorative jar.
- ✓ Small cards or sticky notes.
- ✓ Pens or markers.

Timing:
- ✓ Ongoing, with the jar placed in a central location.

How to conduct the activity:
- ✓ Introduce the gratitude jar and explain its purpose.
- ✓ Provide employees with small cards or sticky notes.
- ✓ Encourage employees to write notes expressing gratitude for their coworkers.
- ✓ Place the notes in the jar periodically.

Trainer Observations:
- ✓ Observe the frequency of notes being added to the gratitude jar.
- ✓ Note the variety and sincerity of the messages.
- ✓ Assess the overall impact on workplace culture.

Prompting Discussion:

- ✓ Discuss the positive effects of expressing gratitude.
- ✓ Encourage employees to share memorable notes or moments.
- ✓ Facilitate a conversation about the importance of acknowledging and celebrating successes.

Application/Learning:

- ✓ Cultivates a culture of gratitude and appreciation.
- ✓ Boosts morale through positive affirmations.
- ✓ Strengthens team bonds through shared expressions of gratitude.

20. Team-building Board Games

Objective:
- ✓ Provide a break from work and encourage relaxation.
- ✓ Promote teamwork and collaboration through board games.
- ✓ Enhance problem-solving and communication skills.

Materials Required:
- ✓ Board games suitable for team play (e.g., Codenames, Pandemic).
- ✓ A designated space for the board game corner.

Timing:
- ✓ Ongoing, with the board games available during breaks.

How to conduct the activity:
- ✓ Set up a designated board game corner with a variety of team-building games.
- ✓ Encourage employees to take breaks and play the games during downtime.
- ✓ Optionally, organize friendly competitions or tournaments.

Trainer Observations:
- ✓ Observe participation levels in the board game corner.
- ✓ Note the level of engagement and enjoyment.
- ✓ Assess the overall impact on team dynamics.

Prompting Discussion:
- ✓ Discuss the benefits of taking breaks and engaging in team-building activities.

✓ Encourage teams to share their experiences with specific games.
✓ Facilitate conversations about the transferable skills gained from playing board games.

Application/Learning:

✓ Provides a break from work and encourages relaxation.
✓ Enhances teamwork and collaboration skills.
✓ Promotes problem-solving and communication in a fun setting.

21. Lunchtime Learning

Objective:
- ✓ Facilitate continuous learning during the workday.
- ✓ Encourage knowledge-sharing among employees.
- ✓ Foster a culture of curiosity and professional development.

Materials Required:
- ✓ Meeting space or virtual platform for sessions.
- ✓ Presentation materials if required.

Timing:
- ✓ Regular lunchtime sessions, scheduled bi-weekly or monthly.

How to conduct the activity:
- ✓ Invite employees to volunteer as presenters.
- ✓ Create a schedule of topics or allow employees to propose subjects.
- ✓ Host short lunchtime sessions where employees share insights on industry trends or new skills.
- ✓ Encourage Q&A sessions to promote engagement.

Trainer Observations:
- ✓ Observe attendance and participation levels.
- ✓ Note the quality of information shared during sessions.
- ✓ Assess the overall impact on employees' knowledge.

Prompting Discussion:
- ✓ Discuss the relevance of the topics presented.
- ✓ Encourage employees to share their thoughts and experiences.

✓ Facilitate conversations about the application of new knowledge in the workplace.

Application/Learning:

✓ Promotes continuous learning during the workday.

✓ Fosters a culture of knowledge-sharing.

✓ Encourages professional development and growth.

22. Desk Plant Adoption

Objective:
- ✓ Enhance the work environment with greenery.
- ✓ Promote a sense of responsibility and care.
- ✓ Contribute to a positive and healthier workspace.

Materials Required:
- ✓ Desk plants or small potted plants.
- ✓ Adoption certificates or labels.

Timing:
- ✓ Ongoing, with plants made available periodically.

How to conduct the activity:
- ✓ Provide a variety of desk plants for employees to choose from.
- ✓ Allow employees to "adopt" a desk plant for their workspace.
- ✓ Provide care instructions for the plants.
- ✓ Optionally, create a display area for adopted plants.

Trainer Observations:
- ✓ Observe the number of adopted desk plants.
- ✓ Note the condition and care of the plants over time.
- ✓ Assess the impact on the overall workspace atmosphere.

Prompting Discussion:
- ✓ Discuss the benefits of having plants in the workspace.
- ✓ Encourage employees to share their experiences with plant adoption.
- ✓ Facilitate conversations about the importance of a positive and green workspace.

Application/Learning:
- ✓ Enhances the workspace with natural elements.
- ✓ Promotes responsibility and care.
- ✓ Contributes to a positive and healthier work environment.

23. Personal Achievements Wall

Objective:
- ✓ Celebrate and recognize employees' accomplishments.
- ✓ Promote a positive and supportive workplace culture.
- ✓ Strengthen team bonds through shared successes.

Materials Required:
- ✓ Bulletin board or designated wall space.
- ✓ Pins or clips for attaching achievements.

Timing:
- ✓ Ongoing, with regular updates.

How to conduct the activity:
- ✓ Designate a space for the Personal Achievements Wall.
- ✓ Encourage employees to pin notes or small items representing their personal achievements.
- ✓ Regularly update the wall to showcase new achievements.
- ✓ Optionally, host brief celebrations for major accomplishments.

Trainer Observations:
- ✓ Observe the frequency of updates on the Personal Achievements Wall.
- ✓ Note the variety and significance of the achievements.
- ✓ Assess the overall impact on workplace culture.

Prompting Discussion:
- ✓ Discuss the achievements showcased on the wall.

- ✓ Encourage employees to share their stories and experiences.
- ✓ Facilitate conversations about the importance of celebrating personal successes.

Application/Learning:

- ✓ Cultivates a positive and celebratory workplace culture.
- ✓ Strengthens team bonds through shared achievements.
- ✓ Promotes a supportive and encouraging atmosphere.

24. Flexibility Day

Objective:
- ✓ Promote work-life balance and employee well-being.
- ✓ Provide flexibility to accommodate individual preferences.
- ✓ Boost morale by offering a unique and employee-centric benefit.

Materials Required:
- ✓ Communication platform for announcing Flexibility Day.
- ✓ Guidelines for employees on how to manage their work hours.

Timing:
- ✓ Periodic, depending on company policies.

How to conduct the activity:
- ✓ Announce Flexibility Day and provide guidelines.
- ✓ Allow employees to choose their work hours or work remotely on this day.
- ✓ Communicate expectations for work deliverables and availability.
- ✓ Encourage employees to share their experiences and feedback.

Trainer Observations:
- ✓ Observe the number of participants on Flexibility Day.
- ✓ Note any impact on productivity and employee well-being.
- ✓ Assess the overall feedback from employees.

Prompting Discussion:
- ✓ Discuss the benefits of flexible work hours.

- ✓ Encourage employees to share their experiences on Flexibility Day.
- ✓ Facilitate conversations about the importance of work-life balance.

Application/Learning:

- ✓ Promotes work-life balance and employee well-being.
- ✓ Demonstrates company commitment to flexibility.
- ✓ Fosters a positive and accommodating workplace culture.

25. Mindfulness Breaks

Objective:
- ✓ Reduce stress and promote mental well-being.
- ✓ Provide employees with tools for relaxation.
- ✓ Enhance focus and productivity.

Materials Required:
- ✓ Quiet space for mindfulness breaks.
- ✓ Optional: Guided meditation scripts or recordings.

Timing:
- ✓ Short breaks scheduled during the workday.

How to conduct the activity:
- ✓ Schedule short mindfulness breaks, e.g., 5-10 minutes.
- ✓ Communicate the availability of the designated quiet space.
- ✓ Optionally, provide guided meditation resources for employees to use.
- ✓ Encourage employees to take mindful breaks at their convenience.

Trainer Observations:
- ✓ Observe the usage of the designated space during breaks.
- ✓ Note any improvements in focus or stress levels.
- ✓ Assess overall feedback on the mindfulness breaks.

Prompting Discussion:
Discuss the benefits of mindfulness in the workplace.
- ✓ Encourage employees to share their experiences with mindfulness breaks.
- ✓ Facilitate conversations about incorporating mindfulness into daily routines.

Application/Learning:
- ✓ Reduces stress and promotes mental well-being.
- ✓ Enhances focus and productivity.
- ✓ Provides employees with tools for self-care and relaxation.

26. Team Playlist

Objective:
- ✓ Foster a sense of community and shared interests.
- ✓ Create a positive and energizing atmosphere.
- ✓ Provide a collaborative and inclusive activity for team members.

Materials Required:
- ✓ Access to a music streaming platform where a collaborative playlist can be created.
- ✓ Speakers or headphones for playing the playlist.

Timing:
- ✓ Ongoing, with the playlist available during breaks or designated times.

How to conduct the activity:
- ✓ Create a collaborative playlist on a music streaming platform.
- ✓ Share the link with team members and encourage them to add their favorite songs.
- ✓ Play the playlist during breaks or designated times.
- ✓ Optionally, rotate the responsibility of curating the playlist among team members.

Trainer Observations:
- ✓ Observe the variety of music preferences represented.
- ✓ Note the impact of the playlist on the team's mood and atmosphere.
- ✓ Assess the level of engagement and participation.

Prompting Discussion:

- ✓ Discuss the diverse music tastes within the team.
- ✓ Encourage team members to share their favorite songs and why they chose them.
- ✓ Facilitate conversations about the role of music in team culture.

Application/Learning:
- ✓ Fosters a sense of community through shared interests.
- ✓ Enhances the team's mood and atmosphere.
- ✓ Promotes inclusivity and collaboration.

27. Office Scavenger Hunt

Objective:
- ✓ Encourage teamwork and collaboration.
- ✓ Foster a sense of exploration and discovery.
- ✓ Provide a fun and interactive team-building activity.

Materials Required:
- ✓ List of scavenger hunt items or clues.
- ✓ Optional: Prizes for the winning team.

Timing:
- ✓ Half-day or full-day, scheduled during a suitable time.

How to conduct the activity:
- ✓ Create a list of items or clues that lead to various locations around the office.
- ✓ Divide employees into teams.
- ✓ Provide the teams with the scavenger hunt list or clues.
- ✓ Set a time limit and have teams race to find all items or solve all clues.
- ✓ Conclude with a debrief and optional prize distribution.

Trainer Observations:
- ✓ Observe teamwork dynamics during the scavenger hunt.
- ✓ Note communication and problem-solving skills.
- ✓ Assess the overall enjoyment and engagement.

Prompting Discussion:
- ✓ Discuss the challenges faced during the scavenger hunt.

- ✓ Encourage teams to share their strategies and experiences.
- ✓ Facilitate a conversation about the importance of teamwork and collaboration.

Application/Learning:

- ✓ Enhances teamwork and collaboration skills.
- ✓ Fosters a sense of exploration and discovery.
- ✓ Provides a fun and interactive team-building experience.

28. Innovation Corner

Objective:
- ✓ Encourage the sharing of innovative ideas.
- ✓ Create a space for brainstorming and collaboration.
- ✓ Foster a culture of continuous improvement.

Materials Required:
- ✓ Designated physical or virtual space for the Innovation Corner.
- ✓ Whiteboard or flip chart for idea visualization.
- ✓ Sticky notes or digital tools for idea submission.

Timing:
- ✓ Ongoing, with regular check-ins or designated review periods.

How to conduct the activity:
- ✓ Dedicate a physical or virtual space as the Innovation Corner.
- ✓ Invite employees to submit innovative ideas, either on sticky notes or through a digital platform.
- ✓ Periodically review and discuss the submitted ideas as a team.
- ✓ Implement and celebrate successful innovations.

Trainer Observations:
- ✓ Observe the frequency and variety of idea submissions.
- ✓ Note the level of enthusiasm and engagement.
- ✓ Assess the impact of implemented ideas on work processes.

Prompting Discussion:

✓ Discuss the innovative ideas submitted to the Innovation Corner.
✓ Encourage employees to share their thoughts on the ideas.
✓ Facilitate conversations about the importance of continuous improvement.

Application/Learning:

✓ Encourages a culture of innovation and continuous improvement.
✓ Provides a platform for sharing and discussing new ideas.
✓ Fosters a sense of ownership and contribution to positive change.

29. Desk Swap Day

Objective:
- ✓ Promote a change of scenery and perspective.
- ✓ Foster new connections and interactions.
- ✓ Enhance team cohesion by breaking down physical barriers.

Materials Required:
- ✓ Communication platform for announcing Desk Swap Day.
- ✓ Optional: Guidelines for employees on how to manage the temporary desk.

Timing:
- ✓ Periodic, based on company policies and preferences.

How to conduct the activity:
- ✓ Announce Desk Swap Day and provide guidelines.
- ✓ Allow interested employees to choose a colleague's desk for the day.
- ✓ Communicate expectations for work deliverables and availability.
- ✓ Encourage employees to share their experiences and feedback.

Trainer Observations:
- ✓ Observe the number of participants in Desk Swap Day.
- ✓ Note any impact on cross-team interactions.
- ✓ Assess the overall feedback from employees.

Prompting Discussion:
- ✓ Discuss the experiences and observations from Desk Swap Day.

- ✓ Encourage employees to share their perspectives on the change of scenery.
- ✓ Facilitate conversations about breaking down physical barriers in the workplace.

Application/Learning:

- ✓ Promotes a change of perspective and a fresh outlook.
- ✓ Fosters new connections and interactions.
- ✓ Enhances team cohesion by breaking down physical barriers.

30. Celebration Wall

Objective:
- ✓ Celebrate and acknowledge personal milestones.
- ✓ Foster a positive and supportive workplace culture.
- ✓ Strengthen team bonds through shared celebrations.

Materials Required:
- ✓ Bulletin board or designated wall space.
- ✓ Pins or clips for attaching celebration notes.

Timing:
- ✓ Ongoing, with regular updates.

How to conduct the activity:
- ✓ Designate a space for the Celebration Wall.
- ✓ Encourage employees to pin notes or small items representing personal milestones.
- ✓ Regularly update the wall to showcase new celebrations.
- ✓ Optionally, host brief celebrations for major milestones.

Trainer Observations:
- ✓ Observe the frequency of updates on the Celebration Wall.
- ✓ Note the variety and significance of the celebrations.
- ✓ Assess the overall impact on workplace culture.

Prompting Discussion:
- ✓ Discuss the celebrations showcased on the wall.
- ✓ Encourage employees to share their stories and experiences.

✓ Facilitate conversations about the importance of celebrating personal successes.

Application/Learning:

✓ Cultivates a positive and celebratory workplace culture.

✓ Strengthens team bonds through shared celebrations.

✓ Promotes a supportive and encouraging atmosphere.

31. DIY Awards Ceremony

Objective:
- ✓ Foster a positive and fun workplace culture.
- ✓ Recognize and celebrate the unique talents and quirks of employees.
- ✓ Strengthen team camaraderie through lighthearted recognition.

Materials Required:
- ✓ Certificates or small trophies for award winners.
- ✓ A venue or virtual platform for hosting the ceremony.
- ✓ Optional: Decorations, snacks, or refreshments.

Timing:
- ✓ Annual or bi-annual, depending on company culture and preferences.

How to conduct the activity:
- ✓ Announce the DIY Awards Ceremony and share categories.
- ✓ Allow employees to nominate their colleagues for various awards.
- ✓ Host the ceremony, either in person or virtually.
- ✓ Present awards with a lighthearted and celebratory tone.
- ✓ Optionally, include entertainment or team-building activities.

Trainer Observations:
- ✓ Observe the level of engagement and enthusiasm during the ceremony.
- ✓ Note the impact on team morale and camaraderie.

✓ Assess the overall feedback from participants.

Prompting Discussion:
- ✓ Discuss the awards presented and the reasons behind each.
- ✓ Encourage winners to share their thoughts and reactions.
- ✓ Facilitate conversations about the positive aspects celebrated in the workplace.

Application/Learning:
- ✓ Fosters a positive and fun workplace culture.
- ✓ Recognizes and celebrates individual talents and quirks.
- ✓ Strengthens team camaraderie through lighthearted recognition.

32. Weekly Wellness Challenges

Objective:
Promote employee well-being and health.
Create a sense of community through shared wellness goals.
Establish healthy habits through small, achievable challenges.

Materials Required:
- ✓ Communication platform for sharing weekly challenges.
- ✓ Optional: Wellness trackers or journals for participants.

Timing:
- ✓ Weekly, with new challenges introduced regularly.

How to conduct the activity:
- ✓ Introduce a new wellness challenge each week.
- ✓ Communicate the challenge details and goals.
- ✓ Encourage participants to share their progress and experiences.
- ✓ Recognize and celebrate achievements at the end of each week.

Trainer Observations:
- ✓ Observe participation levels and engagement.
- ✓ Note improvements in wellness habits and attitudes.
- ✓ Assess the overall impact on employee well-being.

Prompting Discussion:
- ✓ Discuss the challenges and successes of the week.

✓ Encourage participants to share tips and strategies.
✓ Facilitate conversations about the importance of wellness in the workplace.

Application/Learning:
✓ Promotes employee well-being and health.
✓ Creates a sense of community through shared wellness goals.
✓ Establishes healthy habits through small, achievable challenges.

33. Outdoor Meetings

Objective:
- ✓ Provide a refreshing change of environment.
- ✓ Enhance creativity and collaboration during meetings.
- ✓ Promote a healthier work-life balance.

Materials Required:
- ✓ Portable seating arrangements for outdoor meetings.
- ✓ Optional: Notebooks or devices for taking notes.

Timing:
- ✓ Weather-dependent, scheduled during suitable conditions.

How to conduct the activity:
- ✓ Announce the option for outdoor meetings.
- ✓ Schedule meetings to take place in outdoor spaces.
- ✓ Ensure necessary equipment is available for note-taking.
- ✓ Encourage participants to share their thoughts on the outdoor meeting experience.

Trainer Observations:
- ✓ Observe the level of creativity and collaboration during outdoor meetings.
- ✓ Note the impact on participants' energy and engagement.
- ✓ Assess overall feedback on the outdoor meeting experience.

Prompting Discussion:
- ✓ Discuss the benefits of holding meetings outdoors.

- ✓ Encourage participants to share their experiences and preferences.
- ✓ Facilitate conversations about promoting a healthier work environment.

Application/Learning:

- ✓ Provides a refreshing change of environment.
- ✓ Enhances creativity and collaboration during meetings.
- ✓ Promotes a healthier work-life balance.

34. Virtual Escape Room

Objective:
- ✓ Enhance teamwork and problem-solving skills.
- ✓ Foster collaboration among remote teams.
- ✓ Provide a fun and interactive team-building experience.

Materials Required:
- ✓ Virtual escape room platform or software.
- ✓ Communication platform for remote teams.

Timing:
- ✓ Scheduled as a team-building event, either as a one-time activity or periodically.

How to conduct the activity:
- ✓ Choose a virtual escape room platform.
- ✓ Schedule the activity for a specific date and time.
- ✓ Divide remote teams into groups and provide access to the virtual escape room.
- ✓ Facilitate a debrief afterward, discussing teamwork and problem-solving strategies.

Trainer Observations:
- ✓ Observe teamwork dynamics during the virtual escape room.
- ✓ Note communication and problem-solving skills.
- ✓ Assess the overall enjoyment and engagement.

Prompting Discussion:
- ✓ Discuss the challenges faced during the virtual escape room.
- ✓ Encourage teams to share their strategies and experiences.

- ✓ Facilitate a conversation about the importance of teamwork in remote settings.

Application/Learning:
- ✓ Enhances teamwork and problem-solving skills.
- ✓ Fosters collaboration among remote teams.
- ✓ Provides a fun and interactive team-building experience.

35. Gratitude Walk

Objective:
- ✓ Promote mindfulness and gratitude.
- ✓ Provide a break for reflection and relaxation.
- ✓ Foster a positive and appreciative mindset.

Materials Required:
- ✓ Suitable outdoor space for the walk.
- ✓ Optional: Notebooks or devices for jotting down thoughts.

Timing:
- ✓ Scheduled during a suitable time, such as a break.

How to conduct the activity:
- ✓ Announce the Gratitude Walk and encourage participation.
- ✓ Choose a designated outdoor space for the walk.
- ✓ Encourage employees to reflect on positive aspects of work and life during the walk.
- ✓ Optionally, provide prompts or suggestions for reflection.

Trainer Observations:
- ✓ Observe participants' engagement and demeanor during the Gratitude Walk.
- ✓ Note any changes in mindset or mood.
- ✓ Assess overall feedback on the experience.

Prompting Discussion:
- ✓ Discuss the reflections and thoughts from the Gratitude Walk.
- ✓ Encourage participants to share their experiences.
- ✓ Facilitate conversations about the importance of gratitude in the workplace.

Application/Learning:
- ✓ Promotes mindfulness and gratitude.
- ✓ Provides a break for reflection and relaxation.
- ✓ Fosters a positive and appreciative mindset.

36. Collaborative Art Project

Objective:
- ✓ Foster creativity and collaboration.
- ✓ Provide a stress-relief outlet during breaks.
- ✓ Create a shared artistic expression among team members.

Materials Required:
- ✓ Large canvas or art board.
- ✓ Art supplies such as paints, markers, and brushes.
- ✓ Optional: Aprons or protective clothing.

Timing:
- ✓ Ongoing, with the art project accessible during breaks.

How to conduct the activity:
- ✓ Set up a designated area with the art supplies.
- ✓ Communicate the concept or theme for the collaborative art project.
- ✓ Encourage employees to contribute to the artwork during breaks.
- ✓ Rotate the canvas periodically to ensure everyone has a chance to contribute.

Trainer Observations:
- ✓ Observe the level of participation and enthusiasm.
- ✓ Note the variety and creativity of contributions.
- ✓ Assess the overall impact on the workplace atmosphere.

Prompting Discussion:
- ✓ Discuss the collaborative art project during team meetings.
- ✓ Encourage participants to share the stories or inspiration behind their contributions.

✓ Facilitate conversations about the role of creativity in the workplace.

Application/Learning:
✓ Fosters creativity and collaboration.
✓ Provides a stress-relief outlet during breaks.
✓ Creates a shared artistic expression among team members.

37. Storytelling Sessions

Objective:
- ✓ Build connections and understanding among team members.
- ✓ Encourage open communication and sharing.
- ✓ Create a positive and inclusive work culture.

Materials Required:
- ✓ Designated space or virtual platform for storytelling sessions.
- ✓ Optional: Themes or prompts to guide stories.

Timing:
- ✓ Periodic, scheduled during suitable times.

How to conduct the activity:
- ✓ Announce the storytelling sessions and encourage participation.
- ✓ Optionally, provide themes or prompts for storytellers.
- ✓ Allow employees to share personal or professional stories.
- ✓ Maintain a supportive and attentive atmosphere during sessions.

Trainer Observations:
- ✓ Observe the level of engagement and active listening.
- ✓ Note the diversity and impact of shared stories.
- ✓ Assess the overall comfort and participation of employees.

Prompting Discussion:
- ✓ Discuss the stories shared during sessions.
- ✓ Encourage participants to reflect on the lessons or insights gained.

✓ Facilitate conversations about the importance of understanding colleagues' experiences.

Application/Learning:

✓ Builds connections and understanding among team members.

✓ Encourages open communication and sharing.

✓ Creates a positive and inclusive work culture.

38. DIY Ice Cream Bar

Objective:
- ✓ Provide a fun and enjoyable break activity.
- ✓ Boost morale through a shared treat experience.
- ✓ Create opportunities for informal interactions.

Materials Required:
- ✓ Ice cream (various flavors).
- ✓ Toppings such as sprinkles, chocolate chips, and sauces.
- ✓ Bowls, cones, and spoons.

Timing:
- ✓ Occasional or as a special treat during breaks.

How to conduct the activity:
- ✓ Set up a designated area with the ice cream and toppings.
- ✓ Announce the DIY Ice Cream Bar and invite employees to join.
- ✓ Allow employees to customize their ice cream with toppings.
- ✓ Encourage informal conversations during the treat session.

Trainer Observations:
- ✓ Observe the level of participation and enjoyment.
- ✓ Note the variety of ice cream creations.
- ✓ Assess the impact on the workplace atmosphere.

Prompting Discussion:
- ✓ Discuss favorite ice cream combinations during team meetings.
- ✓ Encourage participants to share their experiences during the DIY Ice Cream Bar.

✓ Facilitate conversations about the importance of shared treats in the workplace.

Application/Learning:
✓ Provides a fun and enjoyable break activity.
✓ Boosts morale through a shared treat experience.
✓ Creates opportunities for informal interactions.

39. Fun Facts Friday

Objective:
- ✓ Build connections and create a sense of camaraderie.
- ✓ Promote a positive and lighthearted atmosphere.
- ✓ Encourage team members to learn more about each other.

Materials Required:
- ✓ Communication platform for sharing fun facts.
- ✓ Optional: Themes or prompts for Fun Facts Friday.

Timing:
- ✓ Weekly, scheduled for Fridays or a designated day.

How to conduct the activity:
- ✓ Introduce Fun Facts Friday and encourage participation.
- ✓ Invite employees to share interesting and lighthearted facts about themselves.
- ✓ Share the facts through a designated platform or during team meetings.

Trainer Observations:
- ✓ Observe the level of participation and engagement.
- ✓ Note the variety and creativity of shared fun facts.
- ✓ Assess the impact on team connections and camaraderie.

Prompting Discussion:
- ✓ Discuss the fun facts shared during team meetings.

- ✓ Encourage participants to comment or ask questions about the facts.
- ✓ Facilitate conversations about the importance of lighthearted moments in the workplace.

Application/Learning:

- ✓ Builds connections and creates a sense of camaraderie.
- ✓ Promotes a positive and lighthearted atmosphere.
- ✓ Encourages team members to learn more about each other.

40. Desk De-stress Stretch

Objective:
- ✓ Promote physical well-being and reduce stress.
- ✓ Provide a quick and accessible exercise option.
- ✓ Enhance focus and productivity.

Materials Required:
- ✓ Optional: Small mats or comfortable seating.
- ✓ Instructional materials or a designated yoga instructor.
- ✓ Suitable space for participants to practice desk stretching.

Timing:
- ✓ Short sessions scheduled during breaks or designated times.

How to conduct the activity:
- ✓ Introduce the concept of desk stretching and its benefits.
- ✓ Provide instructional materials or arrange for a yoga instructor.
- ✓ Schedule short desk stretch sessions during breaks.
- ✓ Encourage participants to join and practice the exercises.

Trainer Observations:
- ✓ Observe participation levels and engagement during desk stretch sessions.
- ✓ Note improvements in participants' energy and focus.
- ✓ Assess overall feedback on the impact of desk stretching

Prompting Discussion:

- ✓ Discuss the benefits of incorporating desk stretching into the workday.
- ✓ Encourage participants to share their experiences with desk stretch.
- ✓ Facilitate conversations about the importance of physical well-being in the workplace.

Application/Learning:

- ✓ Promotes physical well-being and reduces stress.
- ✓ Provides a quick and accessible exercise option.
- ✓ Enhances focus and productivity.

41. DIY Desk Games

Objective:
- ✓ Provide a stress-relief outlet during breaks.
- ✓ Foster a sense of fun and enjoyment in the workplace.
- ✓ Create opportunities for short breaks and mental refreshment.

Materials Required:
- ✓ Mini basketball hoops, tabletop games, or puzzles.
- ✓ Optional: Protective coverings for desks.

Timing:
- ✓ Ongoing, available during breaks or designated times.

How to conduct the activity:
- ✓ Provide small desk games in common areas or distribute to employees.
- ✓ Encourage employees to take short breaks and enjoy the games.
- ✓ Optionally, organize friendly competitions or tournaments.

Trainer Observations:
- ✓ Observe the frequency of use and popularity of desk games.
- ✓ Note the impact on employees' stress levels and mood.
- ✓ Assess the overall engagement and participation.

Prompting Discussion:
- ✓ Discuss employees' favorite desk games during team meetings.
- ✓ Encourage participants to share their experiences with the games.

✓ Facilitate conversations about the importance of breaks and stress relief.

Application/Learning:

✓ Provides a stress-relief outlet during breaks.

✓ Fosters a sense of fun and enjoyment in the workplace.

✓ Creates opportunities for short breaks and mental refreshment.

42. Monthly Challenges

Objective:
- ✓ Promote personal and professional development.
- ✓ Create a sense of friendly competition and camaraderie.
- ✓ Establish a culture of continuous improvement.

Materials Required:
- ✓ Communication platform for sharing and tracking challenges.
- ✓ Optional: Prizes or recognition for challenge winners.

Timing:
- ✓ Monthly, with new challenges introduced regularly.

How to conduct the activity:
- ✓ Introduce a new challenge at the beginning of each month.
- ✓ Communicate the details and goals of the challenge.
- ✓ Provide a platform for participants to track their progress.
- ✓ Recognize and celebrate the achievements at the end of each month.

Trainer Observations:
- ✓ Observe participation levels and enthusiasm.
- ✓ Note improvements or achievements during the challenges.
- ✓ Assess the overall impact on personal and professional development.

Prompting Discussion:

- ✓ Discuss the outcomes and experiences of each monthly challenge.
- ✓ Encourage participants to share their strategies and learnings.
- ✓ Facilitate conversations about the importance of continuous improvement.

Application/Learning:
- ✓ Promotes personal and professional development.
- ✓ Creates a sense of friendly competition and camaraderie.
- ✓ Establishes a culture of continuous improvement.

43. Motivational Wall Murals

Objective:
- ✓ Create an inspiring and positive work environment.
- ✓ Foster a sense of pride and identity within the workplace.
- ✓ Enhance the aesthetics of common areas.

Materials Required:
- ✓ Professional artist or muralist.
- ✓ Wall space in common areas.
- ✓ Optional: Materials for touch-ups or maintenance.

Timing:
- ✓ One-time project or periodically, depending on budget and preferences.

How to conduct the activity:
- ✓ Hire a professional artist to create motivational wall murals.
- ✓ Choose themes or quotes that align with the company culture.
- ✓ Schedule the mural creation during a designated period.
- ✓ Unveil the murals and celebrate the enhancement of common areas.

Trainer Observations:
- ✓ Observe the impact of the murals on the workplace atmosphere.
- ✓ Note employees' reactions and engagement with the artwork.
- ✓ Assess the overall feedback on the motivational wall murals.

Prompting Discussion:

- ✓ Discuss the themes and messages portrayed in the murals.
- ✓ Encourage employees to share their thoughts and interpretations.
- ✓ Facilitate conversations about the importance of a positive work environment.

Application/Learning:
- ✓ Creates an inspiring and positive work environment.
- ✓ Fosters a sense of pride and identity within the workplace.
- ✓ Enhances the aesthetics of common areas.

44. Recipe Swap

Objective:
- ✓ Build connections through shared interests.
- ✓ Create opportunities for employees to bond over food.
- ✓ Promote a positive and inclusive workplace culture.

Materials Required:
- ✓ Communication platform for sharing and organizing recipes.
- ✓ Optional: Cooking or tasting sessions for shared recipes.

Timing:
- ✓ **Periodic, scheduled during suitable times.**

How to conduct the activity:
- ✓ Announce the recipe swap and encourage participation.
- ✓ Allow employees to share their favorite recipes through a designated platform.
- ✓ Optionally, organize cooking sessions or potluck events based on shared recipes.
- ✓ Create a recipe collection for employees to access.

Trainer Observations:
- ✓ Observe the level of participation and engagement.
- ✓ Note the variety and creativity of shared recipes.
- ✓ Assess the impact on team connections and camaraderie.

Prompting Discussion:
- ✓ Discuss the recipes shared during team meetings.

- ✓ Encourage participants to share their experiences with cooking or tasting.
- ✓ Facilitate conversations about the importance of shared interests in the workplace.

Application/Learning:

- ✓ Builds connections through shared interests.
- ✓ Creates opportunities for employees to bond over food.
- ✓ Promotes a positive and inclusive workplace culture.

45. Team Photo Day

Objective:
- ✓ Foster team spirit and unity.
- ✓ Create a visual representation of the team's identity.
- ✓ Provide a fun and memorable team-building activity.

Materials Required:
- ✓ Photographer or designated camera.
- ✓ Optional: Props or accessories for creative photos.
- ✓ Suitable backdrop or location for team photos.

Timing:
- ✓ Scheduled as a one-time event or periodically.

How to conduct the activity:
- ✓ Announce Team Photo Day and encourage participation.
- ✓ Schedule a time for the entire team to gather for photos.
- ✓ Optionally, provide props or accessories for creative and themed photos.
- ✓ Share the team **photos with employees and celebrate the experience.**

Trainer Observations:
- ✓ Observe the level of team spirit and enthusiasm during Team Photo Day.
- ✓ Note creative elements and expressions captured in the photos.
- ✓ Assess the overall impact on team bonding.

Prompting Discussion:
- ✓ Discuss the experience of Team Photo Day during team meetings.

- ✓ Encourage participants to share their favorite moments or poses.
- ✓ Facilitate conversations about the importance of team unity.

Application/Learning:

- ✓ Fosters team spirit and unity.
- ✓ Creates a visual representation of the team's identity.
- ✓ Provides a fun and memorable team-building activity.

46. Gratitude Journaling

Objective:
- ✓ Cultivate a positive mindset and workplace culture.
- ✓ Encourage daily reflections on positive aspects of work.
- ✓ Promote overall well-being and mental health.

Materials Required:
- ✓ Gratitude journals for employees.
- ✓ Optional: Writing materials or pens.

Timing:
- ✓ Ongoing, with employees encouraged to journal daily.

How to conduct the activity:
- ✓ Provide each employee with a gratitude journal.
- ✓ Communicate the benefits of gratitude journaling.
- ✓ Encourage employees to take a few minutes each day to reflect and jot down positive aspects of their work.
- ✓ Optionally, organize sessions to share experiences and insights from gratitude journaling.

Trainer Observations:
- ✓ Observe the consistency of journaling among employees.
- ✓ Note any changes in attitude or well-being.
- ✓ Assess the overall impact on workplace positivity.

Prompting Discussion:
- ✓ Discuss the benefits of gratitude journaling during team meetings.

- ✓ Encourage participants to share their reflections and experiences.
- ✓ Facilitate conversations about the importance of cultivating a positive mindset.

Application/Learning:

- ✓ Cultivates a positive mindset and workplace culture.
- ✓ Encourages daily reflections on positive aspects of work.
- ✓ Promotes overall well-being and mental health.

47. DIY Stress Balls

Objective:
- ✓ Provide a hands-on stress relief activity.
- ✓ Encourage creativity and personalization.
- ✓ Promote the use of stress-relief tools in the workplace.

Materials Required:
- ✓ Balloons.
- ✓ Flour, rice, or similar materials for filling.
- ✓ Optional: Decorating materials.

Timing:
- ✓ Conducted as a workshop, scheduled during a break or team-building event.

How to conduct the activity:
- ✓ Provide balloons and filling materials.
- ✓ Instruct employees on how to make their stress balls.
- ✓ Encourage creativity by providing decorating materials.
- ✓ Allow time for employees to create and personalize their stress balls.

Trainer Observations:
- ✓ Observe the engagement and creativity of participants.
- ✓ Note the variety of stress ball designs.
- ✓ Assess the overall impact on stress relief and team morale.

Prompting Discussion:
- ✓ Discuss the experience of making stress balls during team meetings.
- ✓ Encourage participants to share how they use their stress balls.

✓ Facilitate conversations about the importance of stress relief in the workplace.

Application/Learning:
- ✓ Provides a hands-on stress relief activity.
- ✓ Encourages creativity and personalization.
- ✓ Promotes the use of stress-relief tools in the workplace.

48. Inspirational Quotes Corner

Objective:
- ✓ Create a positive and uplifting environment.
- ✓ Provide daily inspiration and motivation.
- ✓ Foster a sense of shared values and purpose.

Materials Required:
- ✓ Designated space for the Inspirational Quotes Corner.
- ✓ Rotating display system or board.
- ✓ Inspirational quotes or messages.

Timing:
- ✓ Ongoing, with quotes changed weekly.

How to conduct the activity:
- ✓ Designate a space for the Inspirational Quotes Corner.
- ✓ Display rotating inspirational quotes each week.
- ✓ Encourage employees to take a moment to read and reflect on the quotes.
- ✓ Optionally, invite employees to submit their favorite quotes for inclusion.

Trainer Observations:
- ✓ Observe the atmosphere and reactions to the displayed quotes.
- ✓ Note any changes in motivation or morale.
- ✓ Assess the overall impact on workplace positivity.

Prompting Discussion:
- ✓ Discuss the impact of the Inspirational Quotes Corner during team meetings.
- ✓ Encourage participants to share their favorite quotes.

- ✓ Facilitate conversations about the importance of motivation in the workplace.

Application/Learning:

- ✓ Creates a positive and uplifting environment.
- ✓ Provides daily inspiration and motivation.
- ✓ Fosters a sense of shared values and purpose.

49. Office Comedy Hour

Objective:
- ✓ Provide a lighthearted and fun team-building activity.
- ✓ Foster camaraderie through shared laughter.
- ✓ Create a positive and enjoyable workplace culture.

Materials Required:
- ✓ Space for hosting the comedy hour.
- ✓ Optional: Microphone or podium for participants.

Timing:
- ✓ Monthly, scheduled during a break or designated time.

How to conduct the activity:
- ✓ Announce the Office Comedy Hour and invite participants.
- ✓ Allow employees to share jokes, funny anecdotes, or humorous experiences.
- ✓ Create a supportive and positive atmosphere for participants.
- ✓ Optionally, invite a comedian to host or perform.

Trainer Observations:
- ✓ Observe the level of participation and engagement.
- ✓ Note the variety and creativity of comedic contributions.
- ✓ Assess the overall impact on team morale.

Prompting Discussion:
- ✓ Discuss the experience of the Office Comedy Hour during team meetings.

- ✓ Encourage participants to share their favorite moments.
- ✓ Facilitate conversations about the importance of laughter in the workplace.

Application/Learning:
- ✓ Provides a lighthearted and fun team-building activity.
- ✓ Fosters camaraderie through shared laughter.
- ✓ Creates a positive and enjoyable workplace culture.

50. Flexible Seating

Objective:
- ✓ Encourage interaction and collaboration among team members.
- ✓ Provide a change of scenery and perspective.
- ✓ Foster a sense of autonomy and choice.

Materials Required:
- ✓ Communication platform for announcing Flexible Seating Day.
- ✓ Optional: Seating arrangements or markers.

Timing:
- ✓ Scheduled as a one-time event or periodically.

How to conduct the activity:
- ✓ Announce Flexible Seating Day and encourage participation.
- ✓ Allow employees to choose their seating arrangements for the day.
- ✓ Optionally, provide markers or indicators for chosen seats.
- ✓ Encourage interactions and collaboration in the new seating setup.

Trainer Observations:
- ✓ Observe the level of interaction and collaboration.
- ✓ Note any changes in the dynamics of team communication.
- ✓ Assess the overall impact on team relationships.

Prompting Discussion:
- ✓ Discuss the experience of Flexible Seating Day during team meetings.
- ✓ Encourage participants to share their observations and insights.

✓ Facilitate conversations about the importance of collaboration and autonomy.

Application/Learning:

✓ Encourages interaction and collaboration among team members.

✓ Provides a change of scenery and perspective.

✓ Fosters a sense of autonomy and choice.

Crafting Tailored Morale-Boosting Activities

Welcome to the empowering chapter of **"Elevate & Energize: *50 Dynamic & Fun Activities for Peak Workplace Morale."*** While the activities presented in this book are diverse and versatile, there's immense power in creating tailored experiences specifically designed to meet the unique needs of your team. This chapter is your guide to becoming a morale-boosting architect, shaping activities that resonate deeply with your team's aspirations and challenges.

Understanding Customization: Unleashing the Power of Personalization

Identify Specific Needs:
- ✓ Revisit the findings from your team's morale assessment.
- ✓ Pinpoint specific areas where targeted morale-boosting efforts are required.

Clarify Objectives:
- ✓ Define clear objectives for your customized activities.
- ✓ Ask: What do you aim to achieve? Improved communication? Enhanced team cohesion? Stress relief?

Consider Team Preferences:
- ✓ Recognize the diversity within your team.
- ✓ Take into account varying interests, work styles, and preferences.

Steps to Craft Tailored Morale-Boosting Activities

Step 1: Brainstorming Session:

✓ Gather a diverse group to brainstorm ideas.
✓ Encourage open dialogue to capture a wide range of perspectives.

Step 2: Align with Company Culture:
✓ Ensure that your custom activities align with the overall company culture.
✓ Reflect on the company's values and mission.

Step 3: Utilize Team Talents:
✓ Leverage the unique talents and skills within your team.
✓ Engage team members in leading or contributing to activities based on their expertise.

Step 4: Budget and Resource Considerations:
✓ Assess available resources, Including time and budget.
✓ Craft activities that are feasible and sustainable in the long run.

Step 5: Test and Iterate:
✓ Pilot your custom activities on a smaller scale.
✓ Gather feedback and make adjustments as needed.

Examples of Tailored Morale-Boosting Activities

Interest-Based Clubs:
✓ Create clubs or groups centered around shared interests, such as book clubs, fitness groups, or hobby circles.

Skill Development Workshops:
✓ Offer workshops that align with the professional development aspirations of your team members.

Employee-Led Celebrations:

✓ Allow team members to take the lead in organizing celebrations for personal and professional milestones.

Flexible Work Arrangements:
✓ Introduce flexibility in work hours or remote work options based on team preferences.

Collaborative Problem-Solving Sessions:
✓ Design sessions where team members collectively address challenges and propose solutions.

Measuring Success and Iterating for Continuous Improvement

Define Success Metrics:
✓ Establish measurable criteria for success.
✓ This could include improved team satisfaction scores or increased participation rates.

Gather Feedback:
✓ Regularly collect feedback from team members.
✓ Use surveys, focus groups, or casual conversations to assess the impact.

Iterate Based on Feedback:
✓ Adjust activities based on the insights gathered.
✓ Be open to experimentation and continuous improvement.

Your Role as a Morale Architect

In this chapter, you've discovered the power of customizing morale-boosting activities to suit the unique needs of your team. As you embark on this journey of crafting tailored experiences, remember that you're not just organizing activities; you're architecting moments that elevate the spirit of your team. Your role as a morale architect is to create an environment where each team member feels seen, valued, and inspired.

Now, armed with insights from your team's assessment and the tools for customization, let's transition to the concluding chapter. It's time to celebrate the transformation you've initiated and set the stage for ongoing success.

Conclusion

As we conclude this journey through **"Elevate & Energize:** *50 Dynamic & Fun Activities for Peak Workplace Morale,"* we hope these pages have sparked a transformation within your approach to team dynamics. The activities shared within this book are not just tools; they are bridges connecting the realms of work and joy, engagement and enthusiasm.

In the realm of human resources and departmental leadership, the pursuit of peak workplace morale is an ongoing endeavor. We recognize that each workplace is unique, with its own culture, challenges, and triumphs. The activities presented here are not one-size-fits-all solutions but rather a diverse array of tools for you to tailor to your team's needs and your organizational ethos.

Our earnest wish is that you find these activities not only practical but also joyful to implement. Morale-boosting should be an experience, not just a task on your to-do list. It's about fostering connections, celebrating achievements, and creating an environment where each member of your team feels seen, valued, and inspired.

Remember, the impact of these activities extends beyond the immediate joy they bring. They contribute to the formation of a resilient, collaborative, and motivated workforce—the heartbeat of any thriving organization.

As you go forth armed with these activities, consider them seeds. Plant them in the fertile ground of your workplace, nurture them with creativity, and watch as they grow into a vibrant tapestry of team spirit. The success of your organization is intricately woven with the well-being and enthusiasm of your teams. May this book serve as a catalyst for a workplace culture where positivity is not just a goal but a way of life.

Thank you for embarking on this journey with us. May your workplace be forever elevated, energized, and a beacon of inspiration for others.

About the Author
'GERARD ASSEY'

Gerard Assey is a Graduate in Economics, a PGD in Management (HRD) and holds a Doctorate in Leadership. Gerard holds several International Qualifications in Sales, Debt Collection, Training & Teaching, and is a 'Fellow' of the prestigious 'Institute of Sales & Marketing Management'-UK, a Certified NLP Practitioner, a 'Certified Trainer', an 'Accredited Management Teacher-Behavioral Sciences', a 'Certified Competency Facilitator', a 'Certified Management Consultant'- (the International credentials of a professional management consultant, awarded in accordance with global standards of the ICMCI); and a Certification from the University of Michigan in 'Successful Negotiation: Essential Strategies and Skills'

He is also a Member of the 'National Association of Sales Professionals' backed with several years experience in varied industries, both in India and Overseas. He also holds an 'Etiquette Consultant' Certification from the USA (by Sue Fox, Author of Best Seller: 'Business Etiquette for Dummies'. She has trained some of the top celebrities' world over). He was also a recipient of a scholarship for extensive training in Japan on 'Corporate Management for India'.

Gerard Assey is 'Founder & Chief Corporate Trainer' of the Group: **'Citius, Altius, Fortius Unlimited'**- an organization that **celebrated 20 years of Glorious Service** in 2021, focusing on 3 Core Competencies:

People. Performance. Profit; in functional areas of Sales & Marketing, HR & Organizational Development, covering Recruitment, Training & Consultancy!

Having managed organizations with large Sales Forces in India & Overseas, his specialization cover extensive areas of Sales Training (All levels - Presentation, Negotiation, Key/ Strategic Accounts Management & Managerial Skills for all sectors), Bid Proposal/ Capture Planning/ Management Trainings, Retail Sales, Customer Service & Customer Retention Programs, Training for Prevention & Collection of Debt, Self & Personal Development Programs (Time Management, Teamwork & Team Building, Business Etiquette & Personal Grooming, Leadership & Managerial Skills, People Management Skills, Train-the-Trainer etc), including preparation of Custom-designed Business Manuals for Internal (HR, Induction, and Sales etc) & External use (Instruction, User Manuals).

Gerard has successfully conducted over 6050 Trainings & Workshops (as of Jan '24) all across India, Middle East, Africa, Europe & S.E. Asia. Besides public programs conducted regularly, both in India & Overseas, he has some of the top names as clients whom he services from Single Owners to large Public & Government undertakings, covering all sectors, for their in-house needs.

His website: www.CollectionSkills.com is the only one in this part of the world to be featured in the 'Collections & Credit Risk Magazine-USA' under 'Who's Who in Training' and ranks TOP, along with other websites listed below on most search engines.

Gerard is author of 105 books already (Jan 2024)

A few of our business related books:

1. Bite-sized Bits on Commonsense Management
2. Heart to Heart on Life's Principles'
3. How to become a Successful Manager
4. The Sales Professionals' Master Workbook of S.Y.S.T.E.M.S
5. The Professional Business Email Etiquette Handbook & Guide
6. The Professional Business Video-Conferencing Etiquette Handbook & Guide
7. Professional Presentation Skills
8. Exceptional Customer Service
9. Professional Tele-Marketing Skills
10. Professional Debt Collection Skills
11. The G.R.E.A.T. Sales & Service Workbook
12. Sales Training Advantage for Results (*The Ultimate Sales Training Manual to enable you stand out as a S.T.A.R.*)
13. CEO Daily Planner & Organizer
14. The Sales Professionals' Master Daily Planner
15. The Professional Debt Collector's Master Daily Planner
16. My Daily Planner & Organizer
17. MY EMERGENCY INFORMATION RECORD (Family Emergency & Peace of Mind Planner)
18. The Ultimate Therapist & Counselors Planner and Organizer
19. Building an Ethical Workplace
20. Managing Relationships at Work
21. Managing Business Meetings Effectively
22. Effective Delegation Skills
23. Goal Setting for Success
24. B2B Selling by Email
25. Professional Business Etiquette & Grooming
26. Dining Etiquette & Table Manners
27. Effective Networking Skills
28. Grooming, Etiquette & Manners for Teens, Young Adults & Future Leaders
29. Inter-Personal Skills
30. Get Ready, Get Hired!
31. Selling in a Recession
32. Effective Receivables Management in an Economic Downturn!
33. Real Estate & Property Sales Training
34. Credit Sales & Accounts Receivable Management
35. Selling Skills for Real Estate & Property Advisors
36. Take G.R.E.A.T. C.A.R.E!
37. Spa, Salon & Health Club Selling Skills
38. Selling Travel, Holiday & MICE Services
39. Selling Skills for Spa's, Salons & Health Clubs
40. Retailing in Salons & Spas

Besides regularly contributing to business & trade journals, including international ones such as the 'Creative Training Techniques' and the 'Sales News' of the U.S.A, He is also a member of several prestigious bodies & trade associations, having participated in many Conferences & Workshops in India & Overseas.

Prior to his last assignment of leading & managing a large MNC as head, Gerard had a 3-year stint in the Middle East as a Consultant with a leading British Consultancy Firm.

As the past 'Official Country Representative' for the International Business Award- 'THE STEVIES'-(the business world's own Oscar) for about 4 years- he ensured a few Indian companies that qualify for the same every year!

Gerard can be contacted at:
Email: training@Sales-Training.in,training@CollectionSkills.com
Websites:

> www.Sales-Training.in
> www.EtiquetteWorks.in
> www.CollectionSkills.com
> www.RetailSalesTraining.in
> www.SalesTrainingIndia.com
> www.ManualPreparation.com
> www.TrainingWithPuppets.com
> www.FirstContactAcademy.com
> www.SalesAndMarketingRecruiter.com

Our **TRAININGS** that can help your team

- ✓ **Sales Effectiveness**: Selling Skills for any Sector: Service/ Logistics/ FMCG Realty/ Insurance & Finance/ Media/ SPA's, Health Clubs & Salons/ Key Account Management, Effective Negotiation Skills/ Bid & Proposal Management Skills/ Retail Sales Training: Any Sector (Auto, Jewelry, Clothing, Luxury etc)
- ✓ **Customer Service Skills**-Complaints Handling & Customer Retention
- ✓ **Debt Prevention & Collection Skills**
- ✓ **Etiquette & Grooming**
- ✓ **Leadership & Managerial Skills**
- ✓ **Self & Personal Development Skills**: Presentation Skills/ Effective Communication Skills/Business Proposal Writing Skills/ Problem Solving & Decision Making Skills/ Empowering Secretaries-The perfect PA! (For Secretaries & PA's)/ Effective Time Management/ Teamwork & Teambuilding/ P.R.I.D.E- **P**ersonal **R**esponsibility **I**n **D**elivering Excellence

www.ingramcontent.com/pod-product-compliance
Lightning Source LLC
Chambersburg PA
CBHW071204130726
47998CB00002B/604